Renewing the Mind 2.0

DEVOTIONAL

Casey Treat

Scripture text is taken from the New King James Version (NKJV) unless otherwise specified.

This book is designed to provide accurate and authoritative information with regard to the subject matter covered. This information is given with the understanding that neither the author nor Winters Publishing Group is engaged in rendering legal, professional advice. Since the details of your situation are fact dependent, you should additionally seek the services of a competent professional.

The opinions expressed by the author are not necessarily those of Winters Publishing Group.

Published by Winters Publishing Group

2448 E. 81st suite 5900 / Tulsa, Oklahoma 74137 USA

Book design copyright 2017 by Winters Publishing Group, All rights reserved.

Cover Design by Christian Faith Center

Published in the United States of America

ISBN: 978-0-99761-246-2

    1.   Religion / Inspirational

    2.   Self-Help / Motivational & Inspirational

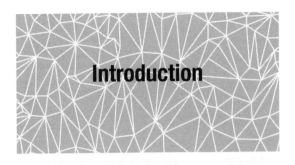

Introduction

If you can change a thought, you can change your life. How many times have you wanted to change but felt unsuccessful? With God, you can have success! In this 30 Day Devotional with Casey Treat, you will be empowered to change with clear and practical steps. These daily inspirations will help you grow in your relationship with the Lord and equip you to be everything God intends you to be. Included in each day is a scripture, renewal thought, and a life-changing prayer!

Day 1

Are You Ready to Change?

Psalm 37:4 "Delight yourself also in the Lord, and He shall give you the desires of your heart."

A lot can happen in 30 days. Bodies can be physically transformed, books can be written, and dreams can be fulfilled. What do you want for the next 30 days? If you are willing to actively pursue God and engage in this with me, I promise you will experience change and renewal in your life. Let's not be too stuck in our habits that we cannot change. We have God living on the inside of us, we have the ability to change and renew!

The next 30 days can be a spark plug to your walk with God, or it can be like any other series of days you have experienced in the past. Make these days count. Since God is a generous God and gives you the desires of your heart, take some time now to set those desires. What do you want? Set some tangible stretch goals for yourself for the next 30 days so that renewal is not only a nice idea but a present reality.

 Renewal Thought: What do you want for the next 30 days? Are you ready to go for it and utilize this time to experience radical growth in your mental and spiritual health? Go for it! God is with you and He will be your strength.

 Prayer: Father, I delight myself in you and I believe you give me the desires of my heart. I pray for divine health, strength, and I pray for my family to be one. I pray for your blessing on my family and career. Thank you God for your goodness and mercy in my life.

Day 2

You Can Change

Joshua 1:9 "Have I not commanded you? Be strong and of good courage; do not be afraid, nor be dismayed, for the Lord your God is with you wherever you go."

Many people wish they could change. Many of us look at our lives and wish things were different – we wish our job was better, our marriage was happier, our future looked brighter. But a wish is not good enough to bring about change. You have to believe that you can change! Once you believe that you can do it, it is possible to move towards it. When my spiritual father, Julius Young, looked at me, newly saved and barely sober, and said to me, "Big Red, you can change," everything began to change. It seems like a simple statement, but in reality those words were life-giving words that birthed hope in me and changed my life.

Today, I say to you that you can change. You are able and you are not alone. Let's walk this journey together, and every day as you study and go through this devotional remember this – you can change. Every area of your life can improve as you continue to renew your mind to the thoughts and ways of God.

 Renewal Thought: Our own self-doubt can be the biggest sabotage agent. Believe that you can change! Believe that you are able and God is calling you to be strong and very courageous in every area of your life.

 Prayer: Father, I believe you are working in me to bring change and renewal. I pray the Holy Spirit will guide me as I walk with you these days. I pray for the courage to go for new things and better things in every part of life. I am not stuck in doubt and fear. I walk by faith into change and renewal.

Day 3

Conformed or Transformed?

Romans 8:1 "There is therefore now no condemnation to those who are in Christ Jesus, who do not walk according to the flesh, but according to the Spirit."

As I was walking through an airport the other day, a person came up to me and said, "Pastor Casey! I love your message on renewing the mind. I have now renewed my mind!" While I appreciated the sentiment, we never are fully done renewing our minds. It is a journey that carries on through the duration of our entire lives! This is not discouraging, if anything, this is a hopeful and exciting gift from God.

There are areas in our lives that if we were to be honest with ourselves, are conformed to the ways of the world. We think, act, talk, and live like the world – that is being conformed to the world. If you have a headache and reach for the medication before confessing healing, that is a simple sign that you are conformed, not transformed. God desires that we be transformed by the renewing of our minds! We don't cover or hide our old way of thinking; we replace it with a new way of thinking.

 Renewal Thought: God doesn't want to patch up your current way of thinking; He wants you to have a whole new way of thinking! This daily process is the journey of a lifetime! What one thought can you change today that will transform your life?

 Prayer: Father, I believe I am on my way to a renewed mind and renewed life. I am taking the steps you give me to become the person you have called me to be. I will not stop, and I will not give up. I am called to be like Jesus and I am walking out that calling every day.

Day 4

Committed to the Process

Romans 8:31-33 "What then shall we say to these things? If God is for us, who can be against us? He who did not spare His own Son, but delivered Him up for us all, how shall He not with Him also freely give us all things? Who shall bring a charge against God's elect? It is God who justifies."

This renewal process is just that, a process! Every pregnant mother understands the importance of process. Every web developer knows the significance of adhering to the necessary steps. As you're in this journey of daily renewal, you may be a new Christian or a longtime person of faith, but we all must follow the process and not give up!

Friendships are a great indicator of our commitment to the renewal process. Who do you spend most of your time with? Are they speaking life over you and encouraging you to be better and achieve greater goals or are they consistently dragging you down? As you're moving through this process of renewal, be brave to evaluate your relationships and gauge which ones are life giving or which ones are holding you back on your process of change.

 Renewal Thought: God has given us all things and equipped us with every tool we could ever need for success in life! Along this process, what tools are you using to further your renewal along and which tools are dull and need to be sharpened or removed?

 Prayer: Thank you, Father, for guiding me in renewal today. I am committed to you and the process of change. I pray for the right people in my life; I pray for godly mentors and friends. I believe wise men and women are walking with me towards new things in my life.

James 4:7 "Therefore submit to God. Resist the devil and he will flee from you."

Jesus was tempted three times by the devil when He was in the middle of a 40 day fast in the wilderness. The devil came when Jesus was at his weakest point physically and tried to dissuade Him. If Jesus was tempted by the devil, don't you think the devil is going to come after you and me as well? As you renew your mind and continue to replace those worldly thoughts with the thoughts of God, the devil is going to do everything he can to distract you and fill your mind with lies and deceit.

James 4:7 says to "resist the devil and he will flee from you." As you are grabbing those thoughts of fear, shame, lack, guilt, sickness and pain, the devil is going to attack your mind. How can you resist the devil? Do exactly what Jesus did in

Matthew 4 – combat the devil's lies with the Word of God. When the thought comes that you are going to fail, remind the devil that God already promised you victory! Every lie of the devil has a coinciding truth from God's Word, so use the Word as your weapon and fight until the devil flees.

 Renewal Thought: The Word of God is our sword (Ephesians 6:17). How can you wield your sword today to combat the devil and resist his lies and attacks?

 Prayer: Father, I submit to you and resist the devil. I refuse to let doubt, fear or negative thoughts steal my faith, strength and renewal. I believe Your Word is true. I am healed, I am free, I am blessed, and I am living the abundant life. I reject the negative thoughts of the enemy and walk in the Word of the Lord.

Day 6

One Thought at a Time

> 2 Corinthians 10:4-5 "For the weapons of our warfare are not carnal but mighty in God for pulling down strongholds, casting down arguments and every high thing that exalts itself against the knowledge of God, bringing every thought into captivity to the obedience of Christ."

It is a crazy idea that we can capture thoughts and make them obedient to Christ. Paul, the author of most of the New Testament must have had an incredible revelation of the mind. With a deep awareness of the Jewish scripture but an ardent rebellion towards his Jewish heritage in his adult years, only to radically turn to Jesus after killing those of the faith, he knew the power of transformation! He knew that Jesus could take a sinful person, filled with thoughts of shame and turn them around to being a mighty Christian that changes their world for Jesus! Do you want to be this type of Christian?

Every thought you have that opposes God's Word, one by one, dismantle it from its place in your mind. Right now, what thought have you had in the last hour that goes against God's best will for your life? Take that thought and "make it obedience to Christ" as Paul instructs in 2 Corinthians 10:5. One by one, you change your world by changing one thought at a time.

 Renewal Thought: Every thought you have takes you on a journey. Is the trajectory of your thoughts leading you where you want to go? Grab every thought and subject it to the Word of God and see as the journey gets better and better!

 Prayer: Father, help me capture every thought that will take away from Your Will for my life. I focus on the thought of Your Word that will guide me to renewal. I believe and trust that Your Word and Your Spirit are guiding me to health, strength, peace and joy. Every other thought is found and cast down. I have the mind of Christ and the purpose of God coming to pass in me.

Day 7

What Is Your Heart Saying?

Proverbs 23:7 "For as he thinks in his heart, so is he. 'Eat and drink!' he says to you, but his heart is not with you."

Who do you say that you are? I say that I am a father, husband, friend, and so forth. These various titles grant me access to certain roles. I call my daughter on the phone, she says, "Hi Dad! Want to go get lunch?" Why? Because she knows I am her dad and want to be around her and spend time with her. Decades of relationship building has shown my loyalty to her and our continual relationship.

God says that you are His child. God says that He perfectly created you to be like Him and that you were created for relationship with Him. Has God given you a title and ownership of something that you are not accepting as yours? When I spend time with my daughter, we know it's because we want to spend time together and hang out! We enjoy each other's company and we embrace the gift of the relationship we have built. God has created us for relationship with Him! Do you realize that you are a son or a daughter of God? When He says you are chosen and loved, accept that in your heart and allow it to define you.

 Renewal Thought: Your thinking determines your lifestyle. You are who you think you are, and your behavioral patterns will reflect who you believe you are. Today, embrace who God says you are. Know that He has qualified you and calls you His child.

 Prayer: Thank you, Father, for a new identity. I am your son/daughter. I am a child of God, a child of the King! I pray to walk with you every day. I believe that my relationship with you is close and strong. I am who you say I am, and I can do all you say I can do.

Day 8

The Power of a Seed

> Genesis 3:1-5 "Now the serpent was more cunning than any beast of the field which the Lord God had made. And he said to the woman, 'Has God indeed said, "You shall not eat of every tree of the garden?"' And the woman said to the serpent, 'We may eat the fruit of the trees of the garden; but of the fruit of the tree which is in the midst of the garden, God has said, "You shall not eat it, nor shall you touch it, lest you die."' Then the serpent said to the woman, 'You will not surely die. For God knows that in the day you eat of it your eyes will be opened, and you will be like God, knowing good and evil.'"

Sometimes all the devil has to do to derail you is place a tiny seed of doubt in your mind. Then, you water it and nurture that seed until it is a full grown tree in your mind! The devil placed a seed of doubt in Eve's mind and instead of grabbing that thought and combating it with God's Word, she watered it and nurtured it which led her to sinning against God. The seed is powerful because, although it starts small and seemingly insignificant, it grows into something much more impactful.

A seed is easily ignored as inconsequential in the magnitude of our lives because we don't see the tree when we see the seed. What seeds have you allowed to take root in your mind that you need to uproot right now? Are there some spindly trees that you can prohibit from growing any more by uprooting them now? Take action and don't allow them to grow any further!

 Renewal Thought: Just as a negative seed has the power to grow into an unhealthy harvest in our lives, so too does the positive seed! Sow seeds today of faith and hope in your mind today. Remind yourself who you are in God and who He says that you are!

 Prayer: The seeds of health, prosperity, peace and joy are working in me. Father, I believe Your Word is growing in me and will produce good fruit. I am rooted and grounded in Your Love, Strength, Favor and Blessing. Your seed is growing a great harvest in my life. The harvest of the healthy and new relationships, prosperity, and peace are growing in me. Thank you, God!

Casey Treat

Day 9

Think About What You're Thinking About

Philippians 4:8 "Whatever things are true, whatever things are noble, whatever things are just, whatever things are pure, whatever things are lovely, whatever things are of good report, if there is any virtue and if there is anything praiseworthy—meditate on these things."

How many times in a week do you think about what you are thinking about? Thoughts run through our minds at a rapid speed! We think about 100 things at one moment or we seek to completely clear our minds the next. But do we ever stop and critically evaluate what we're thinking and how long we are spending on each thought?

How long do you spend thinking about coffee in the morning? How long do you spend thinking about your financial woes? It may be a fleeting thought, but if it comes to your mind throughout the day, those build up like dams that block the thoughts of God from coming to you. To think the thoughts of God, evaluate what else you're spending time thinking on and then replace those thoughts. An honest evaluation might be just the right next step for your growth towards renewing your mind!

 Renewal Thought: Paul tells us to think on whatever is noble, pure, and lovely. Think about what you're thinking about and find ways to focus on that which is noble, pure, and lovely.

 Prayer: Father, thank you for a clean mind and Godly thoughts. I'm thinking on those things that help me every day. The thoughts of Your Word are keeping me strong and at peace today. I pray that I hear the Holy Spirit and keep His truth on my mind.

Day 10
Faith That Makes You

Matthew 9:22 "But Jesus turned around, and when He saw her He said, 'Be of good cheer, daughter; your faith has made you well.' And the woman was made well from that hour."

Jesus is constantly telling us through the Gospels that what we believe will come to pass! If we can change our thoughts, we can change our lives. If we can believe it, we can receive it. This isn't about naming and claiming something that isn't meant for us or is against the will of God. This is about claiming what God has promised is ours to have! Healthy bodies, sound minds, loving families, and generous lives that bless others are all promises of God for every one of us. Is your faith active to believe God for those things to be yours? Just as a baker makes a cake with the right ingredients, you are making your life. Be intentional to use the right ingredients of faith.

The woman who touched the hem of Jesus' garment in Matthew 9 did all she could to get to Jesus. Although she was condemned to total isolation unless clearly identified, she risked her life with an act of bravery and Jesus accredited her greatly by saying that her faith healed her! What is your faith doing for you?

 Renewal Thought: God has given you great authority in your life through faith. You can change your life as you start believing you are able. Put your faith to work and believe that God wants you to be healed and whole in every way.

 Prayer: Father, I pray for new thoughts that will bring me to new places. I pray Your Word will be big in my mind so my faith will grow stronger and stronger. Thank you, Father, for leading me beyond doubts and fears. Faith is working in me. I believe that I receive all your promises to me.

Day 11

Your Highest Calling

Romans 8:29 "For whom He foreknew, He also predestined to be conformed to the image of His Son, that He might be the first-born among many brethren."

DNA is a powerful element in our genetic makeup, and it has become popular to do family history research into the scientific makeup of one's past. While this is a great tool for your health and wellness, it cannot overshadow the Word of God. Just because you were born with a specific makeup does not change that God says you can live according to His promises. Sure, you were born that way; we were all born into the sinful world. But God says that we can be renewed to His perfect will and were predestined to be conformed to the image of His Son! What an amazing promise.

Most times we believe what has been told to us for many years. "You have a history of mental illness" or "you have an addictive personality" or "everyone in our family struggled with diabetes" are repeated statements that go undetected in the fabric of our conversations. We anticipate calamity to befall us and act surprised when it does. This is not God's best, and we can change this pattern of thinking! Your highest and truest calling is to be like Christ. You were created to be like Him, and anything out of alignment with that truth must be removed from your life.

 Renewal Thought: Your truest self is to be like Christ. Your highest calling is to be like Jesus Christ and walk in His promises. Anything outside of this should be subjected to the Word of God and renewed.

 Prayer: Thank you, Father, for the new faith that is growing in me. I am a new person, with a new heart and a new mind. I pray you are leading me to new life in every way. I am not bound to the failures of my past. Thank you, God, for the blood of Jesus that gives me a new spiritual DNA. Health, strength and success in life are in my future. I believe You are working in me.

Day 12

Work It Out

Philippians 2:12 "Therefore, my beloved, as you have always obeyed, not as in my presence only, but now much more in my absence, work out your own salvation with fear and trembling."

Jesus came to bring salvation to all people. Every single person on the planet is invited into intimacy with God through Jesus Christ. The way to that is what we call "salvation." Jesus came so that all might be saved (1 Timothy 2:4). This salvation, although an open invitation and a completely free gift, must be "worked out," Paul explains to the church in Philippi.

What happens when you work something out? It starts to become toned, stronger, and better equipped for performance. When you first work out your arms, their performance level is low. But as you build strength, they are able to lift more weight. How can you work out your salvation? Paul is encouraging us to not just get saved and maintain the same lifestyle. We are to get saved and then begin to get stronger in the Word of God, stronger in prayer, and stronger in the spiritual disciplines that God has invited us into.

 Renewal Thought: You are given abilities and power to grow in every area of life. How can you work out your salvation today and become stronger as a Christian? Don't give up after one attempt. Keep building your muscles and refining the gift of salvation.

 Prayer: Father, I pray you are working in me to work out my salvation. I believe I have the energy and wisdom of the Holy Spirit to work out Your Will for me in every realm of life. I believe You lead and guide me every day as I work out my salvation and find all You have for my life.

Day 13

The Higher Way

Isaiah 55:9 "For as the heavens are higher than the earth, so are My ways higher than your ways, and My thoughts than your thoughts."

We all have a way of doing things. We generally follow a series of patterns for getting ready in the morning, a series of patterns throughout our day at work, and an order we stick to every evening. When something comes in and messes up the pattern, it can cause discomfort and chaos in our day. But when we want to see a change in our lives, we have to disrupt these patterns and habits and make small changes that will result in a big shift!

The prophet Isaiah writes that God's ways are far superior to our ways. What patterns or habits can God help you perfect that would literally shift your life and take you from frustrated or complacent to victorious, excited about the future, and joyful in your life? We have access to God's ways through the presence of the Holy Spirit.

 Renewal Thought: As you go about your day today and this week, ask the Holy Spirit what patterns and habits you are carrying out that are not helpful and ask God to help you show you His higher ways.

 Prayer: Thank you, Father, for the higher thoughts and higher ways that You have for me. I repent of the lower life and seek after the high life of Your perfect will. I pray You help me see when I am walking into a lower way and help me stay on the high way of life. Your ways are higher than mine, so I pray You keep me in Your Way.

Day 14

Every Stubborn Thought

Proverbs 4:23 "Keep your heart with all diligence, for out of it spring the issues of life."

We have all witnessed the child in the grocery store that is stubborn and wants to have something the parent is unwilling to give. We watch as the parent tries to train their child that just because they want something, doesn't mean they can have it! What are we watching when parents are engaged in this process? It is a battle of wills, and the parent is trying to show that their way is the right way and the one that will prevail.

When we want to live selfish and destructive lives, the Word of God is showing us the way to live right. Just because we want that thing doesn't mean we should have it, and just because we had the thought doesn't mean it was good and beneficial. We can grab thoughts and throw them out. When the thought crosses your mind that is negative, destructive, or damaging, put it against the truth of God's Word and watch what happens.

 Renewal Thought: Areas in my life where I am stuck reveals a truth in the Bible that I do not fully believe. Are you having stubborn and destructive thoughts? Find a scripture that speaks to that issue and confess that scripture over your life.

 Prayer: Lord, I repent of the stubborn thoughts and behaviors that have kept me down. I turn away from every thought that will stop the flow of Your Blessing in my life. I pray, God, for the grace to change and renew my mind. I pray You are leading me to new life in every way.

Day 15

How Did This Happen?

Hebrews 4:12 "For the word of God is living and powerful, and sharper than any two-edged sword, piercing even to the division of soul and spirit, and of joints and marrow, and is a discerner of the thoughts and intents of the heart."

Everything starts with a thought. Every moment, every choice, every major and minor action starts first in the mind and then is carried out into our lives. When we find ourselves in the middle of a tragedy, an affair, in sin and problems, we feel surprised and shocked at ourselves. We ask ourselves, "How did this happen?" The truth is, it started with a seed thought that we didn't capture and grew into something we never intended it to be.

Is there an area in your life where you're asking yourself how you got there, how you let it get so bad or so out of control? You are not alone, and there is a way to get out!

Today, you are half way through this renewal devotional, and it is time to get down to business! It is time to start making some changes that can change your current situation and take your life to the next level. You got to the place where you now are through thinking a certain way and embracing certain thoughts. You can get yourself out in the same way. Use the Word of God to start cutting away that which doesn't need to be in your life. The Bible is your sword, and you have the power to refine.

 Renewal Thought: Use the Word of God to trim away everything that doesn't belong in your mind. Capture those worldly thoughts, cut them down, and remove them from your mind.

 Prayer: Father, I pray for the strength and passion to press for Your perfect Will in every part of life. Let me not settle for mediocrity but may I reach for the high calling of God in Christ Jesus. Thank you, Holy Spirit. You will keep me going through all the obstacles I face, and You will help me live this blessed life.

Casey Treat

Day 16

Go-To Thoughts

Philippians 4:19 "And my God shall supply all your need according to His riches in glory by Christ Jesus."

We can renew our mind day by day and continue to get better, but when tragedy hits our thoughts can run wild! We hear a bad report, see something terrible on the news, or get a negative text, and suddenly our thoughts begin to spiral out of control.

When I was diagnosed with Hepatitis C, the doctor gave me a series of very scary reports all boiling down to early death for me. This is a time where my thoughts could have easily spiraled out of control! However years prior, I started implementing go-to thoughts and creating a habit of confessing scripture the moment I heard bad reports. At the moment of tragedy, I practiced speaking life. I started with the small issues so when big issues arose, I had already practiced my response. Before implementing positive go-to thoughts, I would have allowed my mind to spiral out of control. But I avoided that pitfall, and so can you.

Do you have some go-to scriptures that can become your go-to thoughts? If not, today is your day to pick a few. A good one is Philippians 4:19. Anytime the devil tries to attack your mind, family, health, career, or any area of your life, remind yourself that God will meet and supply every single one of your needs! There is a higher thought, and that is the thought you can go to.

 Renewal Thought: Your mind is going to go to what is comfortable and familiar in times of tragedy. Set your habits now for when hard times come so you can be ready and comfortable confessing scripture over your life.

 Prayer: Father, help me to be strong when the storm comes against me. I pray I will believe when everything seems dark. I trust You, Holy Spirit, to guide me through the valley of the shadow of death. I know Your Word is true even when I face hard times. I pray the thoughts of God will lift me above the negatives of this world. I believe, Lord, when I am weak Your grace makes me strong.

Casey Treat

Day 17

Breaking Out of Your Comfort Zone

Lamentations 3:22-23, "Through the Lord's mercies we are not consumed, because His compassions fail not. They are new every morning; great is Your faithfulness."

Our strongholds give us a sense of familiarity and comfort. Like that pair of jeans you always throw on, strongholds can be the most comfortable thought you have. You have thought it so many times that you don't even realize the thought is there!

For instance, do you expect to get sick at least once a year? You just expect it so when it happens, you aren't surprised and you just embrace it as the change of season. You don't even realize the stronghold of sickness in your mind because maybe your parents always said it, now you always say it, and it's a fixture in your mind.

There are many things we automatically believe that have constructed strongholds in our minds. Break out of those comfortable thoughts today! You don't have to be sick. You don't have to have a terrible day, you don't have to have a bad marriage, and your children don't have to go through "a bad phase."

 Renewal Thought: The Lord loves you and wants you to live an abundant and prosperous life. Begin to see His love and embrace His goodness in order to help you break free from the comfort zones that ensnare you.

 Prayer: I pray the Truth of God is making me free from the strongholds that hold me down. I believe that negative expectations will not control my marriage, career, finances, or health. I am transformed by the renewing of my mind to experience God's perfect Will. I thank you, Father, for healing and strength, peace and joy. I am pulling down strongholds and walking in Your Favor.

Day 18

The Walk To Freedom

John 8:31-32, "Then Jesus said to those Jews who believed Him, 'If you abide in My word, you are My disciples indeed. And you shall know the truth, and the truth shall make you free.'"

Many times, we make choices that are motivated by our fear. We need the money, so we stay in a job we dislike. We don't want to get overweight, so we eat healthy. We don't want to feel guilty, so we go to church. These choices all reflect our fears instead of hope. What would happen if instead of operating in fear, you operate in faith?

Making choices rooted in faith brings freedom. We are no longer stuck in a job we hate but see the job as a blessing and a training ground for the better career that is to come. We no longer see the grilled chicken and vegetables as a bland meal but as sustenance for a healthy life. We go to church with the mindset that we don't *have* to go, but we love to go and are strengthened in the community of believers. Perspective changes everything!

 Renewal Thought: Your freedom is connected to your perspective on things, and shifting perspective will help you see God's truth at work in your life.

 Prayer: Father, I pray that faith and hope will guide my thoughts and decisions. I believe, God, that You empower me to rise above the negatives and live the abundant life You came to give me. With Your help, Father, I doubt my doubts and believe my beliefs. I believe renewal is working in me and abundant life is mine.

Day 19

Why Do You Like What You Like?

Matthew 12:35 "A good man out of the good treasure of his heart brings forth good things, and an evil man out of the evil treasure brings forth evil things."

We all have a natural inclination for certain things. Why do we like what we like at the restaurants we go to? We don't normally sit down and ask ourselves why we favor chicken over pork, we just do. We don't know why we love certain songs, we just do.

We have talked a lot about habits, patterns, and the outpouring of what is already within coming out and manifesting in our lives. Jesus shows us in Matthew 12 that the good person brings forth good things. This is a harsh verse because what if everything that is coming out of your life is bad? The good thing is that we have been on this daily journey of renewal, and that which is bad is changing and being renewed to God's Word.

As you change and renew your mind, you start to see the outpouring of that goodness. Your thoughts are in alignment with God's Word, and your speech follows. Then because your speech has changed, your conversations and relationships start to change. This domino effect is exactly the process Jesus was speaking to and shows us how powerful it is when we renew our minds and change that which flows out of us.

 Renewal Thought: You like what you like for a reason. Continue to put God's thoughts into your daily life and start to see what you like and desire become a reflection of Godliness.

 Prayer: Father, I ask that you would change the things I like. Renew the things that are normal to me. I am no longer satisfied with the taste of this world. I long for and love the Bread of Life, the peace of God, and the love of the Holy Spirit. Renew my diet, Lord; change my tastes that I will love all you have for me.

Day 20

God Loves You For You

Romans 5:8 "But God demonstrates is great love towards us, in that while we were still sinners, Christ died for us."

On day twenty, I think it is important to pause in our active pursuit of renewal and growth to remind you that God loves you. He is proud of you and loves you just as you are today. Even on your worst days, even in the midst of the worst sin and shame, God loves you and desires a personal and intimate relationship with you.

I know I can get so wrapped up in the steps to change that I forget to pause and remember God's endless love for me. If I never did change, if I failed one hundred more times, that cannot and will not change God's love for me. Hating yourself and being hard on yourself won't help you and is not what God wants for your life. He loves you and wants to see you prosper in every area of your life.

 Renewal Thought: Change must come from a positive emotion. Embrace God's love for you and remember how proud He is of you. This will enable you to desire to know Him and be like Him more.

 Prayer: Thank you, Father, for loving me and accepting me just as I am, no matter what my weaknesses and problems are. You are for me, and you love me unconditionally. I believe the passion of the Holy Spirit is moving me. I will not give in to guilt or condemnation but desire to see God's best in every part of life. Thank you, Father, for your goodness towards me.

Day 21

Who's Really in Charge Here?

Deuteronomy 30:19 "I call heaven and earth as witnesses today against you, that I have set before you life and death, blessing and cursing; therefore choose life, that both you and your descendants may live."

While most relationships start based on feelings and emotions, any long-standing marriage was sustained by choice. Emotions enrich our lives and add dimension, but they do not add structural support. Many people say that they need to follow their feelings. We sing songs about listening to our heart, having a loving feeling, and being enraptured in the moment. While they make catchy lyrics, they do not help us live Godly lives.

What do you allow to be in control of your life? If your emotions dictate the majority of your day, your days may look more like a rollercoaster than a journey with God. Emotions cannot control your life; choices must control your life. Choices set upon God's Word are stable, unwavering, and a strong structural support to build your life on.

 Renewal Thought: What emotions have been running your life that you are realizing are unfruitful? How can you change from being emotionally driven to setting your mind on Godly choices and staying committed to them?

 Prayer: Today, Father, I choose life and I choose blessing. I choose to believe and not doubt. I choose to walk by faith, not fear. With your help, Holy Spirit, I will choose all that God wills for me. I believe abundant life is mine, and I am taking the steps required to experience it to the fullest. Thank you, God, for the power to choose. I choose life and I choose blessing today.

Day 22

Lessons from Thomas the Train

2 Timothy 1:7 "For God has not given us a spirit of fear, but of power and of love and of a sound mind."

When Julius said to me, "Big Red, you can change," I really didn't know if I could. I wanted to. I hated the life I was living and was ashamed of who I was, but I didn't know if I actually could change. I saw the way my parents lived, and I thought that was all that was ahead of me. I didn't know if I could have a loving marriage. I didn't know if I could have a job I enjoyed. I doubted every positive scripture and message I heard.

I say that because you might be in that same place or you may know someone who is in that spot right now. The Bible doesn't make these claims to mock us. The Bible doesn't say that we are strong and able to live victorious lives purely to poke fun at our insecurities and inadequacies. The Bible tells us these things because we are able! You may not fully believe me yet, but you can change. You can go a day without being angry, or swearing, or going to the bottle for solace. It may seem impossible now, but just like that little blue engine that could, you can do more than you think because you have more than enough on the inside of you empowering you and strengthening you to win.

 Renewal Thought: God has given you strength and boldness on the inside of you! You are able to win with God on your side. The greatest source of strength lives in you, and that power is yours for the taking. Even through our unbelief, keep trusting that you are able.

 Prayer: Thank you, God, for the spirit of power, love and a sound mind. I pray the spirit of fear will have no place in my life. You did not give me a spirit of fear, so I refuse to be controlled by it. I pray Your power and love will lead me and all I do. My life, my spouse, and my children are free from fear; we walk in the Spirit of God.

Day 23

Seek and Find

Jeremiah 29:13 "You will seek me and find me when you search for me with all your heart."

You know when you start liking a certain car or brand how you start to see it everywhere? It is crazy how we overlook things every day until we have an interest in them, and then those things become all we see. The prophet Jeremiah said that when we seek the Lord, we will find Him. The same principle applies here as it does with anything we seek. When you start looking, He will start to become all you see!

It doesn't do us any good to want a better life but keep it as a distant hope or a far-fetched wish. We cannot treat God like a magic genie. God wants to be sought after and desired. When we seek Him and want Him in our lives, God eagerly responds and is present with us in all things. Although God is omnipresent and is everywhere and always with us, we still need to seek Him and desire His presence with us. When we seek Him, it allows Him to be at work in our lives.

 Renewal Thought: When you allow God to be at work in your life, you will begin to see His goodness and provision in every area of life. Seek Him today and watch how you see Him everywhere and in everything.

 Prayer: Father, I hunger and thirst after Your presence in my life. I long for Your truth, and I desire Your will in all I do. Thank you, God, that You give me the desires of my heart. I believe those who hunger will be filled, those who seek will find. Those who desire Your blessing will not be disappointed.

Day 24

The Path You Choose

Joshua 1:8 "This Book of the Law shall not depart from your mouth, but you shall meditate in it day and night, that you may observe to do according to all that is written in it. For then you will make your way prosperous, and then you will have good success."

Life is filled with choices, and the choices you make determine the path you will take. People like to say that God is in control, and while God is in control of the cosmos, He has given you control of your life and given you the ability to choose the life you live. As you are going about your day today, be aware of the choices you make. How are you spending your time? What is consuming your thoughts? These choices may seem small in the moment, but they are directing your life.

If you don't like the path you are on, redirect! God Word is our GPS and when we get off course, we can connect to God's Word and find the path that we want to be on. Just like when you are trying to find a new location, you trust the GPS for direction, so it is with God. We are going somewhere we have never been and must use God's guidance to navigate. We cannot look at the world to get us where we want to go; they don't know how to get there! God's Word is our ultimate guide and will take us safely to our destination.

 Renewal Thought: God's Word aligns us to perfection. It cannot derail us and cannot misguide us. Revisit the goals of renewal you set at the beginning of the month. How can you make sure you are on track and following the guide of His Word?

 Prayer: Thank you, Father, for the grace of change in me. I pray by the power of the Holy Spirit I can make my way prosperous and I will find good success. I believe Your Word is working in me. Your Word is true in every part of my life. I keep Your Word in my heart, mind, and mouth. I observe to do all that You have written.

Day 25

Finding the Balance

Ecclesiastes 3:1 "To everything there is a season, a time for every purpose under heaven."

Matthew 11:28-30 (The Message) "Are you tired? Worn out? Burned out on religion? Come to me. Get away with me and you'll recover your life. I'll show you how to take a real rest. Walk with me and work with me—watch how I do it. Learn the unforced rhythms of grace. I won't lay anything heavy or ill-fitting on you. Keep company with me and you'll learn to live freely and lightly."

When we look at God's creation, it is clear that God is a God of order. When we study the human anatomy, we see the creative balance God has fashioned perfectly. There is order and balance built into everything God has created, and yet sometimes we live our lives completely out of balance and order. This way of living is contrary to God's way.

An easy example of living out of balance is to ask yourself how many times you have felt too tired or too busy for something important. Are you worn out and tired but feel trapped to keep up with the life you feel obligated to live? Living with God is to live in balance and assurance in Him.

Renewing your mind to be like Christ is not to add more burden to your life – it is to do the exact opposite. It is to make room in our minds and lives for God. When we do that, we discover the balance we have been seeking all along.

 Renewal Thought: Does your life feel like a circus, featuring one juggling act or another? Do you feel overwhelmed by life or under-whelmed and disappointed? Neither are God's best. Find balance in God today and walk in His grace for your life.

 Prayer: Father, I pray that the peace of God that passes all understanding will guard my heart and mind through Christ Jesus. I rest in you, Lord, and believe you are working all things for my good. When I feel anxious and nervous, I rest in You alone. I trust you, Lord, to find good things to pass to me. I refuse to be stressed and under pressure. I walk in Your timing and rest in Your peace.

Casey Treat

Day 26

The Extra Mile

Daniel 1:20 "And in all matters of wisdom and understanding about which the king examined them, he found them ten times better than all the magicians and astrologers who were in all his realm."

I love the story of Daniel! I love that he stood out from the rest of the people because he had an excellent spirit. Daniel inspires me to do the little things that make a big difference. Out of all the stories in the Bible, Daniel's story isn't marred with a single moral failure. The book of Daniel shows time and time again that Daniel rose to the top due to his relationship with God and his excellent spirit.

Jesus died for the world, but He will not compromise to be in it. He is different and is constantly calling us out of the world to be different! Daniel never fit in, nor did he try. He knew that his excellence glorified God and that was what he sought after. Your excellent spirit glorifies God and causes you to be elevated above others. Keep pursuing God's thoughts and God's ways and you will have an excellent spirit.

 Renewal Thought: Be excellent not for attention but to glorify God. You serve an excellent God, and when you are excellent you are being Christ-like.

 Prayer: Lord, I believe I am on my way to greater things in life. I pray my marriage, children, and career are rising with Your excellent spirit. I pray, Father, I am not stuck being average or mediocre. You make me better, Lord. Your excellent spirit is moving me upward in all I do.

Day 27

What Do You Want?

Mark 10:51 (The Message)
"What can I do for you?"

In Mark 10, Jesus asked a blind man what he wanted. This question almost seems to be mocking the man, as it appears evident that the man would want his sight. But Jesus asked him for a reason. Your desires reflect your heart and invite God to work on your behalf. Just because it seems evident that something would help you doesn't mean God can give it to you.

Do you want it bad enough to keep pressing toward it? Do you want the life God has for you, or are you willing to get complacent and accept where you are right now? The difference between mediocre and great is desire. What do you want, and do you want it bad enough to continue to ask God for it, seek His will, and stay diligent until you have it?

Renewal Thought: Don't give up on a dream just because it hasn't happened yet. Keep seeking God and let the desires of your heart be made known to Him! Our God is a good God and wants to give you what you ask of Him.

Prayer: Energize my desires, Lord. Help lift my vision and my faith. Let me not be satisfied but help me reach for Your perfect Will. I believe my desires and dreams are coming to pass. I delight myself in You, Lord, and you are giving me the desires of my heart.

Day 28

Keep Going, You are Closer Than You Think

Numbers 14:18 "The Lord is longsuffering and abundant in mercy, forgiving iniquity and transgression; but He by no means clears the guilty, visiting the iniquity of the fathers on the children to the third and fourth generation."

Sometimes we just give up too soon! Don't quit and get tired when the reward is right on the other side! One of the traits of God is that He is longsuffering. He is patient and committed to the process. This is a good trait to pick up now that we are coming to the close of our 30-day devotional. Are you committed to the process and willing to keep going? Don't give up; results are closer than you think!

You are better, stronger, and further along in the journey than you may be giving yourself credit for. Stay committed to these principles and remember that God is on your side. He is fighting for you and wanting you to succeed in every area of your life. As you capture negative thoughts and continue to prayerfully change from worldly thoughts and patterns to Godly ways, you will keep shifting the course of your life. Don't give up too soon!

 Renewal Thought: Every captured thought and every time you take a step in the right direction, the devil wants to pull you back and whisper lies of discouragement. Don't listen to the lies of the enemy but listen to God's voice of love and faith in you.

 Prayer: Thank you, Father, for the strength to keep going. I refuse to give up or give in. I believe You have abundant life for me, and I am running the race to win the prize. I pray, Holy Spirit, you strengthen and energize my life to keep going and to receive all you have for me. I am strong in the Lord; I am on my way.

Day 29

Everything Hangs on This

Matthew 22:37 "Jesus said to him, 'You shall love the Lord your God with all your heart, with all your soul, and with all your mind. This is the first and great commandment. And the second is like it: "You shall love your neighbor as yourself." On these two commandments hang all the Law and the Prophets.'"

Have you ever tried to hang a photo on the wall with one nail and realized the photo was too large and kept tilting to one side? Trying to renew your mind and live a Godly life without loving God and loving yourself will continue to cause you to tilt the wrong way. You will repeatedly struggle if you keep forging ahead but failing to love as Jesus teaches us to.

My challenge to you today is to love yourself and the unique qualities that make you who you are. You were fearfully and wonderfully made, and

God made you perfect! Everything hangs on your ability to love God and love others as you love yourself. Being truly renewed according to God's Word means that you have a Godly self-image and know the value you have in Christ.

 Renewal Thought: The more you value something, the better you will treat it. You are priceless to God and His prized creation. Believe that about yourself and value yourself as God's finest handiwork.

 Prayer: Father, I believe Your love flows in my life. I love you. I love those around me and I love the person You are making me to be. I believe Your love never fails. I am moved by the love of God that is shed abroad in my heart by the power of the Holy Spirit in me.

Day 30

The Daily Renewal

> Romans 12:2 "And do not be conformed to this world, but be transformed by the renewing of your mind, that you may prove what *is* that good and acceptable and perfect will of God."

Renewing your mind is a daily pattern and way of life. To grab those pesky negative thoughts and change them for the thoughts of God is a habit you may have only just begun! Your journey ahead is going to be the best days of your life. I truly believe that the best is yet to come for you. God has such incredible things in store for you as you continue to renew your mind and life to the thoughts of God.

As you continue to renew your mind, you continue to walk in the perfect will of God and your life reflects the goodness of God to the world. One small change today can make a big difference in

your life tomorrow. I encourage you to keep going! Keep grabbing those thoughts and subjecting
them to the Word of God and watch as your life
continues to go from glory to glory.

 Renewal Thought: My friend, you can
change!

 Prayer: Lord, I believe renewal is working in
me. I am on my way to Your perfect Will. I
pray, Father, you will continue to lead and
guide me to truth and renewal. I want Your
Will to be at work and evident in every part
of my life. I believe you are working in me
and great things are ahead of me.